BEETHOVEN

The Choral Fantasia

final section with English words by Robert Elkin

Order No: NOV 070046

NOVELLO PUBLISHING LIMITED

CHORAL FANTASIA
FINAL SECTION

English words by Robert Elkin*

BEETHOVEN
Opus 80

Allegretto, ma non troppo (quasi Andante con moto)
Cominciando il pezzo si dà un segno al core delle voci

© Novello & Company Limited 1964
19283

4

earth. Peace on earth and heart's con - tent - ment are the
Licht, äuss - re Ru - he, inn' - re Won - ne herr - schen

earth. Peace on earth and heart's con - tent - ment are the
Licht, äuss - re Ru - he, inn' - re Won - ne herr - schen

boons which men hold dear: Lo! the
für den Glück - li - chen, Doch der

boons which men hold dear: Lo! the
für den Glück - li - chen, Doch der

[cresc.]

sun - shine of the Mu - ses brings these bless - ings ev - er
Kün - ste Früh - lings - son - ne lässt aus bei - den Licht ent -

sun - shine of the Mu - ses brings these bless - ings ev - er
Kün - ste Früh - lings - son - ne lässt aus bei - den Licht ent -

19283

SOPRANO *f* Full
Oh, the blos - som - ing of beau - ty when the
Gro - sses, das in's Herz ge - drun - gen, blüht dann

ALTO *f* Full
Oh, the blos - som - ing of beau - ty when the
Gro - sses, das in's Herz ge - drun - gen, blüht dann

TENOR *f* Full
near. Oh, the blos - som - ing of beau - ty when the
stehn. Gro - sses, das in's Herz ge - drun - gen, blüht dann

BASS *f* Full
near. Oh, the blos - som - ing of beau - ty when the
stehn. Gro - sses, das in's Herz ge - drun - gen, blüht dann

f Orch.

heart to truth as - pires! ___ When a soul is high up -
neu und schön em - por, ___ hat ein Geist sich auf - ge -

heart to truth as - pires! When a soul is high up -
neu und schön em - por, hat ein Geist sich auf - ge -

heart to truth as - pires! ___ When a soul is high up -
neu und schön em - por, ___ hat ein Geist sich auf - ge -

heart to truth as - pires! When a soul is high up -
neu und schön em - por, hat ein Geist sich auf - ge -

10

19283

ceive, ye no-ble spi - rits,   all the gifts by Mu-sic
hin, ihr schö-nen See - len,   *froh die Ga-ben schö-ner*

ceive, ye no-ble spi - rits,   all the gifts by Mu-sic
hin, ihr schö-nen See - len,   *froh die Ga-ben schö-ner*

ceive, ye no-ble spi - rits,   all the gifts by Mu-sic
hin, ihr schö-nen See - len,   *froh die Ga-ben schö-ner*

ceive, ye no-ble spi - rits,   all the gifts by Mu-sic
hin, ihr schö-nen See - len,   *froh die Ga-ben schö-ner*

Solo   Orch.

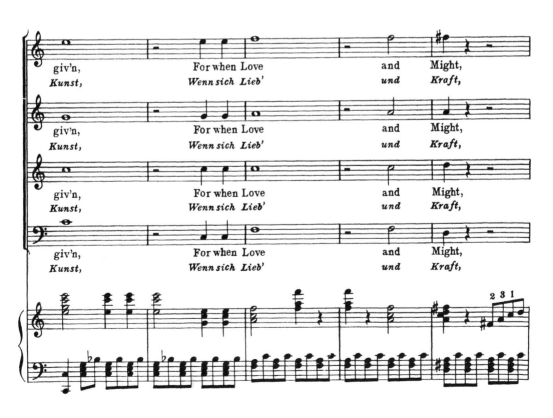

giv'n,   For when Love   and   Might,
Kunst,   *Wenn sich Lieb'*   *und   Kraft,*

giv'n,   For when Love   and   Might,
Kunst,   *Wenn sich Lieb'*   *und   Kraft,*

giv'n,   For when Love   and   Might,
Kunst,   *Wenn sich Lieb'*   *und   Kraft,*

giv'n,   For when Love   and   Might,
Kunst,   *Wenn sich Lieb'*   *und   Kraft,*

16

19283

20

high - est Heav'n, Man is near to high - est Heav'n,
Göt - ter-gunst, lohnt den Men - schen Göt - ter-gunst,

high - est Heav'n, Man is near to high - est Heav'n,
Göt - ter-gunst, lohnt den Men - schen Göt - ter-gunst,

high - est Heav'n, Man is near to high - est Heav'n,
Göt - ter-gunst, lohnt den Men - schen Göt - ter-gunst,

high - est Heav'n, Man is near to high - est Heav'n,
Göt - ter-gunst, lohnt den Men - schen Göt - ter-gunst,

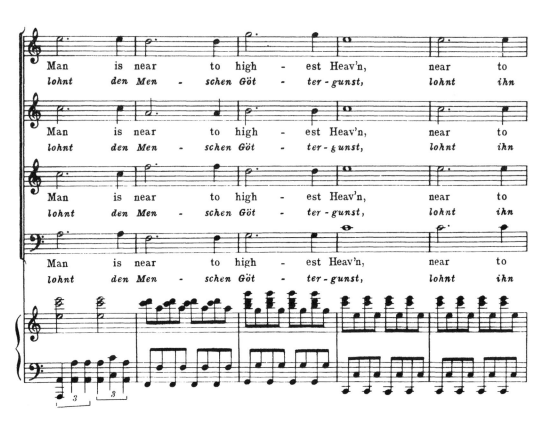

Man is near to high - est Heav'n, near to
lohnt den Men - schen Göt - ter-gunst, lohnt ihn

Man is near to high - est Heav'n, near to
lohnt den Men - schen Göt - ter-gunst, lohnt ihn

Man is near to high - est Heav'n, near to
lohnt den Men - schen Göt - ter-gunst, lohnt ihn

Man is near to high - est Heav'n, near to
lohnt den Men - schen Göt - ter-gunst, lohnt ihn

Printed and bound in Great Britain by
Caligraving Limited Thetford Norfolk

3456789